# Reiki Gyosei Waka
# Imperial Meditation Poetry

## by Owen Bruhn

Contains poetry by Emperor Meiji (1852-1912), Empress Consort Shoken (1850-1914) as well as selected poems by Dr Ainslie Meares (1910-1986).

United with the world,
the clear moon shines deep within—
knowing it is there
in undisturbed stillness-
this alone completes my ease.
Chosei Hoshii, Shingon Priest, Late Heian Period[1]


What could be more poetic
Than the healing
Of body and mind?
Ainslie Meares[2]

1 *Yo to tomo ni kokoro no uchi ni sumu tsuki o ari to shiru kosa hatruru narikere in* Goshuish Imperial compilation. Kokoro no uchi ni refers to fudoshin ie.stillness.
2 Meares A (1985) A Way of Doctoring. poem 3, pg4

By Owen Bruhn. Author & Publisher.
ISBN: 978-0-6481084-7-4

**Dedication**

To my teachers & colleagues.

**Disclaimer**

This book is intended for general information only. It must not be used as a substitute for learning in person from a qualified competent teacher. Nor must it be used as a substitute for consulting a qualified health practitioner. Nor can the author and publisher accept any responsibility for any person attempting to apply general information presented herein. The reader takes on complete responsible for applying information in this book. Reader responsibility includes, but is not limited to, all responsibility for themselves plus affected third parties not limited to family and carers. The views expressed herein are those of the author and publisher. They do not represent nor necessarily reflect the views of others.

# Table of Contents

# Preface

I was fortunate to learn Stillness Meditation from Dr Ainslie Meares (1910-1986). I've been involved, one way or another, ever since 1984. Decades earlier, Meares put forward his theory that hypnotic and meditative states consist of a universal state hidden underneath a variable overlay (aka phenomena). The underlying state being a Still mind. Absence of overlay reveals Stillness. Over the years, Meares visited many systems all over the world. He verified his theory and looked for anything else that might benefit his patients.

When Ainslie Meares visited Japan, Reiki was only practised in secret. In Australia, Reiki had not yet arrived. After I finished my book about teaching Stillness Meditation, I began to visit other meditative touch therapy systems he had not. Reiki has let me look at Stillness Meditation from the outside in (and vice versa). Both systems have a lot in common (see Ch 8-9). For example, poetry is part of Meares' system. In Usui Mikao's time, and later in the Reiki that stayed in Japan, waka were recited in class. Yet poetry is absent in Reiki that left Japan and spread via Hawayo Takata worldwide. When I heard about Reiki waka I was intrigued.

I am grateful to be able to share a collection of more than 100 translated waka, background on how they passed into Reiki and how you might fit waka into your practice. This book includes 82 waka by Emperor Meiji plus 24 by his spouse, Empress Shoken. I also share examples of Ainslie Meares' poetry and a bit about his system too.

**Most people will do well to read this book in order**. Ch. 8 will provide fresh insights into your Reiki practice from a different angle. Ch. 9 explains how poetry and meditation are related. This may have greater application than you think right now.

**If you just want to read waka**: go to Ch 4-5, read a couple of waka daily. The following waka are often presented in collections (Ch 4 (3, 4, 19, 22, 24, 26, 27, 42, 58, 75) & Ch 9 (103-106)). Ch 6 has one line summaries that may help with tricky ones.

**If you find waka hard to read.** Read Ch. 8-9 and then try the poetry at the end of Ch. 9. After further practice you should find reading waka easier. If not, consider revisiting waka later on. For the time being, this will allow more time on other aspects of your practice where you can see benefits accruing.

Owen Bruhn 2025

# 1. About Emperor and Empress

## Emperor Meiji (Meiji Tenno)

Emperor Meiji (1852-1912) was the 122nd Emperor (Tenno) of Japan. His reign began in 1867 when Japan was opening up to the world. It was a time of immense change. Great change happened in government administration, religion, the economy and this was reflected in many aspects of Japanese life. Meiji Tenno sought to preserve his nation's culture and identity,  whilst encouraging friendship with other countries and facilitating the introduction of Western culture and technology. He began writing poems (waka) around 8 years old and composed over 90,000 during his lifetime. That's 5 waka a day for 50 years. Meiji Tenno ruled and this made his waka **Gyosei** (literally, song or poem made by Emperor).

After an early rebelllion, Meiji Tenno was informed by his military advisors that he could not write love waka to avoid encouraging further problems. No prohibitions were placed on his wife, Empress Shoken. Otherwise, their waka expressed their thoughts and feelings on many topics, including Japan, the people and their own reflections. Many of their waka emphasize Shinto values (see Ch. 2).

# Empress Shoken

Empress Shoken (1850-1914) married and became the consort of Meiji Tenno in 1869. She supported the Emperor and especially promoted national welfare and women's education. She worked to support women, in Japan and elsewhere: *"family prosperity depends on feminine foresight... Thus, prosperity is the basis of the progress of human society... we must realise the importance of the responsibilities incumbent on woman.[3]"*

Towards the end of her life she donated money to the International Red Cross and this fund continues on till this day.

Outside of Japan, few people know that the Empress wrote waka, her first when she was 5 years old. She[4]: *"devoted numerous long hours to... her favourite occupation, the composition of waka... She alone enriched the forty thousand waka existing at that time by no less than 1,090 new poems".* Others say she wrote up to 30,000 waka. There have been at least 8 regnant Empress of Japan ie who ruled rather than married the ruler. Empress Shoken did not rule and so her waka are not Gyosei.

Next, we discuss how Meiji Gyosei became part of Reiki.

---

3 Model Women by Empress Shoken. A booklet cited in 4.
4 The Empress Shoken Fund. Int. Review. Red Cross Fund. pp518-529. 1963.

© O Bruhn

# 2. Meiji Tenno Gyosei and Reiki

During Meiji Tenno's reign great changes occurred in Japan. Christianity was allowed back into Japan and Shinto replaced Buddhism as the national religion. About 1,500 years ago, the first Emperor claimed descent from the Sun Spirit. This continued and Meiji Tenno was both head of State and Shinto. State-Shinto violently suppressed sects\groups seen to challenge its authority eg. Omoto in 1921 and Honmichi in 1926. People involved in Reiki, like Usui Mikao, had to tread lightly to avoid State Shinto displeasure.

There is a long link of 1,000 years between Zen and Samurai culture. Several Navy Officers became students of Usui Mikao. Some say that the influx of Navy Officers was due to a medical shortage on naval vessels (eg. learning Reiki would help things like lack of space, equipment or few medical doctors). Others say that these Officers introduced Gyosei to avoid State concerns and preserve Reiki. Some go further - perhaps some of them had been tasked by the State to steer Reiki along a path that avoided conflict with it. However you look at it, reciting Gyosei in class was a win-win. It acknowledged the Emperor, had benefits and allowed Reiki to flourish.

Gyosei are waka written by a ruling Emperor. Meiji Tenno wrote Gyosei but passed away a decade before Usui's began teaching Reiki at his School (Gakkai). Meiji's son Yoshihito ruled until 1920 when he became ill. Hirohito (Yoshihito's son) became Regent and then Emperor in 1926 after Yoshihito passed away. Neither Yoshihito nor Hirohito wrote waka.[5] Meiji's Gyosei were widely disseminated. The State promoted waka in general and heavily promoted Meiji Gyosei to facilitate national identity, loyalty, patriotism and moral resolve. In Samurai and pre-Meiji culture, waka were composed to express such qualities and enhance group coherence. The Samurai tradition of waka recitation was taken up by the Meiji military forces. That influx of Navy Officers coincided with the new practice of reciting Gyosei at start of class. The year Usui Mikao passed away, *Gyosei Hyakushu* ("100 Gyosei") was published with 2 Admirals listed amongst the 3 compilers. Over time the number and order of Gyosei varied from 125 down to only a few.[6] Substantial changes occurred in updated Reiki Gyosei Booklets after World War 2 ended. By then, Gyosei were absent from the Reiki that left Japan via Takata Hawayo.

---

5 Yoshihito wrote Chinese poetry. Hirohito wrote some waka in the 1980s.
6 Tomita (1933). Reiki to Jinjutsu. Tomita Ryu-Teate Ryoho.

© O Bruhn

Usui Mikao's memorial stone says: *"when guiding people, one must first have them internalise [Ikun] the ethical testament left by the late Emperor Meiji and recite the 5 Precepts morning and evening, so that these take root in their hearts and minds."*[7]

The memorial then discusses the precepts in detail.

**Ikun** refers to testament left by a person who has passed away. A will, the bible and a judge's decision are all forms of testament. Some say Ikun might mean the Imperial Rescript on Education. The Rescript emphasised patriotism, loyalty and morality. Adults in Japan who attended school from 1890 onwards had to recite it each school day and could recite it from memory. By 1926, the year Usui passed, most of the population (ie all those under 56 yrs old) could already recite the Rescript from memory, without Reiki classes.

Usui's Reiki School classes in Japan involved reciting Gyosei, Precepts, meditation, Reiju (attunement) and healing partner work[8]. Ikun refers to Gyosei rather than the Rescript. The term Ikun showed respect for Meiji Tenno and Usui Mikao. Admiral Ushida, 2nd President, Usui Reiki Association did the calligraphy for the memorial stone. He was also one of the compilers of *Gyosei Hyakushu (100 Gyosei booklet).*

## About This Poetry Collection

The original hand written Meiji Tenno Gyosei and Shoken waka are sacred due to the State-Shinto connection and are closely guarded. Only a few hundred have ever been made public.

This book presents a collection of more than 100 translated waka. This includes 1 Gyosei in Ch. 3, 77 in Ch. 4 plus 4 in Ch. 9. This selection presents a complete range. A few Gyosei presented (eg. patriotic ones) might not work so well for meditation today.

Ch. 5 contains 24 waka by Empress Shoken. Today, one might read Shoken Waka or other poems in one's practice. Ainslie Meares wrote Zen like verses designed to be accessible for western people. Some examples are included later in this book. Ch. 9 also discusses the use of poetry in Reiki and within the Stillness Meditation system.

The next chapter provides information about poetic aspects of waka and its translation using a single Gyosei example.

---

7 Yue ni sono hito o oshieru ya, mazu Meiji Tennō no ikkun o hōtai shi, chōseki gokai o tonaete kokoro ni nen seshimu.

8 *Reiki Ryoho Hikkei-* Gakkai Shuyokai

# 3. Waka Translation

## Waka Poetry in General

The Japanese **waka**, has 31-syllables. It is a precursor to haiku, which has 17. Waka (aka **tanka**) verses are arranged in 5 lines in an alternating pattern of 5-7-5-7-7 syllables adding up 31. Syllables but not rhyming are a critical part of waka.

The first waka poetry was written 1,000 years before the Meiji Era. There was a long tradition of waka composition and reading.

Meiji and Shoken waka were recorded in Japanese writing. Meiji Gyosei went into Reiki in that form so they could be read by Japanese people. Modern people reading Waka must consider a few things. First, the non-Japanese speaking reader must rely on translation of calligraphy, language and ideom (culture) to capture the English meaning. Second, time passing since Meiji's reign has built in further changes to the meaning of some words and their recording due to standardisation and simplification of Japanese writing that occured around 1945.

Understanding some basic concepts helps to get the poetic impression. Although you don't really need to get too bogged down in theory. If you read some waka you will become familiar with these elements. Some points are listed below in no particular order.

**Nature and the seasons**. Waka often reflect upon the beauty and changing nature of the seasons. Often depicting seasonal landscapes and fleeting moments in nature.

**Spiritual themes** and the human condition are explored.

**Everyday living**. They may also reflect upon emotions and nuances of daily experience.

**Parts**. Waka are often divided into two parts. The first sets the scene or theme. The second provides a conclusion or twist. The first 5- syllable line sets scene and the remaining 4 lines (-7-5-7-7) reply. A two line comment (5-7-) and 3 line reply( -5-7-7) is also common. Parts may be absent in some observational waka. Others may seem to have 3 parts eg observation and 2 part reply.

Sometimes, several waka were used together like verses in conventional poetry. Uncommonly, more complex forms were utilised. Aside from waka 90-91 (Ch. 4) the translated waka in this book are in the conventional 5-7-5-7-7, 31 syllable format.

**Uta Makura** are standard poetic names of events or locations with natural beauty or historical associations eg. Yoshino for its cherry trees and their beautiful transient blossoms. Yamato and Shikishima refer to Japan. There are many others.

**Hansei** is self-reflection and growth. It is a key component of continuous improvement (Kaizen). The process involves consideration of the past with an attitude of "no mistakes, only identification of better ways". We can't change the past but we can often find better approaches. Cycles of experience, learning and growth often with an element of humility. Very Reiki.

**Ma** is "the space between". On Ma, Ainslie Meares writes[9]: *"In Japanese art, the idea of "the space between" refers to the relationship of the different elements of the work. Thus the elements of the work are given new meaning by considering how they stand in relationship to each other. But there is more to it than this. "The space between" comes to have significance in its own right. It has meaning of its own. In this way the Japanese masters convey ideas of distance and closeness. There is significance in absence as well as in presence. In one way "the space between" is empty and silent, but at the same time, it surrounds us all, and so unites and brings us together. It pervades the art of Japan. It is seen in many forms: in Japanese painting, in the art of flower arrangement, in the tea ceremony, and in the arrangement of the great stones in the temple gardens."* Spatial, temporal and sensory aspects of the space between are important in both waka and Stillness Meditation teaching.

**Kotodama** means the spirit that dwells in words. Words can profoundly influence people and the world around them. Kotodama emphasises the sounds and emotional impact above the language meaning. They are said to come from ancient times when ancestors relied on sound spirit with few or no words at all. Kotodama are said to foster harmony, understanding, and change.

In Stillness Meditation, a short verbal guiding and some nonverbal phonation are part of Stillness Meditation class although most of the facilitation is by touch. Kotodama and nonverbal phonation have a lot in common.

An experimental kotodama translation is at the bottom of pg16. It retains the vowel sounds but at a cost. The words are far more vague. There is no other way. Remember, kotodama depends upon sounds rather than the meaning of words.

92 of the waka in Japanese are in Ch. 7. Some of them could also be spoken aloud if you wish to experience kotodama that way.

---

9 Meares A (1969) J Clin Exp Hyp. 15(4):156-159.

# One Waka, Many Translations

Below is a famous Meiji Tenno Gyosei[10] and several translations.

**Original**

| | |
|---|---|
| Yomo no umi | (5) |
| mina hara kara to | (7) |
| omou yo ni | (5) |
| nado nami kaze no | (7) |
| tachi sawaguramu | (7) |

**Word-by-Word**

Yomo- all directions; Umi- sea.
Mina- all; hara-origin or womb; kara- shared source.
Omofu- think\believe; yo ni-in the world.
Nado-why; nami- waves; kaze- wind.
Tachi- rise; sawaguramu- in uproar; ramu- might.

**Literal translation**

The seas in all directions
All from the same origin
Then why do the waves and wind
As I believed
Rise and clash in such turmoil?

**Poetic**

Though all seas are one,
born from the same wide womb,
Why then do wind and wave
rise up in restless strife?

---

10 Kokumin Shinbun Newspaper 7 Nov 1904; No 17 in Gyosei Hyaku 1926; No 121 in Gyosei Hyaku Juu Ni Go 1991; Ogawa F (1986) Everyone can do Reiki..

## Modern 5-7-5-7-7

| | |
|---|---|
| I thought all oceans | (5) |
| came from the same place — | (7) |
| so why are the waves | (5) |
| and winds always fighting, | (7) |
| like they don't even know each other? | (7) |

You can see that one Waka can be translated in many ways. But, it is the poetic impression that is important. These translations all evoke a similar feeling. Read a few waka and you will know what I mean. Further discussion on poetry in Reiki and Stillness Meditation is in Ch. 9. The theory will give you some ideas but only reading poetry will evoke a meaningful experience.

Below is the highly experimental kotodama waka mentioned earlier.

### "Kotodama Waka"

| | |
|---|---|
| Go, slow boat, moonlight. | (5) |
| Still, magic lava glows. | (7) |
| Hope flows through your mind. | (5) |
| Mad fox barks, sang, then no. | (7) |
| Clap it, hammer, thump and drum. | (7) |

The 1911 translation by Lloyd,[11] a Missionary living in Japan, was entitled "the muttering of the storm". It has a different feel to those above. Same waka many translations.

My heart's at peace with all, and fain would I
Live, as I love, in peace and brotherhood:
And yet the storm-clouds lower, the rising wind
Stirs up the waves, the elemental strife
Rages around. I do not understand
Why this should be. T'is plainly not our fault.

In a few instances in Ch 4-5, I have provided a second translation. The second is in italics. For example, see 7 and 7A (in italics) in the next Chapter.

---

11 Lloyd A (1911) The Open Court: V 1911. 9(3).

# 4. Meiji Tenno Gyosei

1. Songs from hearts sincere,
Though heard but once in passing,
Touching souls attune,
Can never be forgotten,
Or lost, however simple.

2. Without a shadow,
Cloudless, floweth ever clear,
The light that shineth
Forth in crystalled words that make
Bright the depth of hearts sincere.

3. The God, who seeth
All things in secret hidden,
The cloudless bosom
Of man, sincere and faithful,
Will flood with light revealing.

4. With the unseen God,
Who see'th all secret things,
In the silence
Communes from the earth below,
The heart of the man sincere.

5. Even to weeping,
The heart of the sincere,
Moveth the bosoms,
Of spirits in peace on high,
Afar from the storms of earth.

6. How swiftly floweth[12]
From its height, the mountain stream!
The very sand-grains
Of its bed in motion seem
Swiftly flowing, flowing free

7. I have no leisure!
Yet 't is sweet, the fleeting thought
From out of chaos
Into order fair to bring,
Shaping songs with feeling fraught.

7A. *I let my thoughts flow as they will— a quiet comfort in a life too busy to find real rest.*

8. The flower of the heart,
Alone by its sweet perfume
In secret distilled,
Embalmeth in fragrance rare
The words of the poet-song.

8A. *On words floating above the surface, what is pleasing— is the flower of a person's heart.*

9. Quickly flowing thoughts
In the garments of fashion to hide
As yet all untrained,
Than the heart of an innocent child
On earth can ought be fairer!

9A. *Still unknown. The thoughts we'll think, The things we'll make. How beautiful is a young heart.*

---

12 Floweth permits 2 syllables which allows the line 5 needed for 57577.

10. Unto the children,
Born in these progressive years
At which we wonder,
First of all the tales of old,
Full of glory, should be told.

11. Behold the baby,
Practicing with zealous care
His letter-writing!
And from him a lesson learn
Effort brings its sure return.

12. The old man leaneth
On his staff - why grieve ye sore !
I would that he should
Totter on, life's hill-slope o'er,
Yet a thousand seasons more.

13.Within the country
Hamlets, God be praised, to-day
Still linger, here and
There, the simple, sweet old ways,
In homes old-fashioned.

*13A. From long ago days,*
*the way old houses were built*
*still quietly stays*
*in the heart of the country,*
*untouched by the flow of time.*

14. Though small his dwelling,
Within that simple, bending dome,
The snail, contented,
Finds an ample space for home,
Scorning not his station.

15. All study scorning,
Think not now your tasks are done!
Your parchments given
Prove the strife is but begun,
Though to- day your hearts are proud.

*15A. Child you've been given a second chance, a
clean page- don't turn away from the path of
learning. Now, walk onwards.*

16. The dust that floateth
In the air, slow settleth down,-
A weight that lifts not
From the shoulders, once so strong,
Bending now beneath their wrong.

*16A. As it gathers,
The task of clearing it seems too hard,
Though it was once merely specks of dust,
It now feels like it has become
a pile hard to sweep away.*

17. The hands that measure
Time, perchance may feebly falter!
And man, misguided,
Err, his charted course to alter,
Taking wrong for righteousness.

18. Or high or lowly
Be thy station, 'tis thine own
Thy best is duty.
Do it then without a moan,
Thereby making life sublime.

19. Resent not Heaven,
Nor on others cast the blame.
Thyself consider,
And behold the fault which springs
From the heart of secret things.

20. Like the morning sun,
In beaming brightness climbing
Up the eastern sky,
The mind[13] of man should ever
Shine forth in cloudless splendour.

21. High in the heavens,
Above all earth-born shadows,
Soareth the skylark,
With music sweet alluring
The hearts of longing mortals.

*21A. Drawn by longing,*
*my heart drifts upward-*
*toward the eternal heavens,*
*where hope takes wing*
*as the skylark rising.*

---

13 or "the heart of man" or "heart- mind"

22. Even to the summit
Of mountains that rise on high
Into the heaven,
A pathway ascendeth,
Alone by the climber gained.

23. The burden of snow,
The wild blast of the storm-wind,
Give dignified grace
To the pine tree that bravely
Through the strife so long standeth.

24. Beneath the eaves
Where the trickling raindrops
The stone is hollowed!
Seeing that, the hardest task
Possible appears at last.[14]

25. Long are the years,
The days and months of waiting,
While we ever strive,
Our cherished purpose seeking
To realize completely.

25A. *Long stretch the years-*
*days and months of waiting,*
*as we press onward,*
*seeking to fulfil at last*
*a deeply held purpose.*

---

14 Last line can also be read: "*Seems possible at last*".

26. Amid the grasses,
That to us seem filthy weeds
By careful seeking,
Oft' o'er-shadowed by the reeds,
Healing herbs of grace are found.

27. The lustreless gem,
In its whiteness, despise not,
Forgetting the fact
That your hand the hard labour
Of its polish neglected.

28. In peace remember
That of old the gods did rule
With bow and arrow!
And the noble arts of war
Cherish still in honour high.

*28A. The one entrusted by the gods to govern the land- even in peace, must not become complacent.*

29. Though ye are girded
No more with the gleaming sword
Ready for battle,
Forget not, in idle sloth,
Yamato's[15] keen soul to whet.

30. Along the mountain,
Where maples skirt the pathway,
Lest whip should injure
The bending brilliant branches,
I' ll curb my restless steed.

---

15 Yamato is the area where the first Emperor ruled. Also, a King Arthur like figure.

*30A. If I crack the whip*
*on a maple tree branch*
*it will surely shake*
*holding back my skittish horse*
*on the road to the hills.*

31. Brave with holy zeal,
In mortal strife desist not!
Yet, howe'er thou strike
The foe who wrongs thy country,
In wrath remember mercy.

*31A. For our countries sake*
*foes who bring hostility*
*even if crushed*
*should be shown compassion*
*do not forget this matter.*

32. Whene'er -I sorrow,
Thinking of our soldiers slain
In bloody battle,
In my soul I grieve the more
For their parents weeping sore.

*32A. For the country's sake*
*he fell- yet still a parent*
*cannot help but weep,*
*holding in their silent heart*
*grief no honour can erase.*

---

33. No lip should falter,
But to lip repeat the names
Of those who offered
Life for country's sake, that
Here may live forever more.

*33A. As the ages pass,*
*let their story be retold —*
*those noble in heart,*
*who laid down their precious lives*
*for the sake of our homeland.*

34. Looking at the moon,
I stand on my verandah!
Yet, e'en there my thoughts
Fly forth to fields of battle!
How fare my valiant soldiers!

*34A. Even in stillness,*
*gazing at the quiet moon,*
*my heart drifts again —*
*imagining the battle*
*and the field where brave men fell.*

35. Swiftly pass the hours,
While unheeding still I sit
Late into the night,
Talking of the men who died
Bravely for their country-side.

36. Unto the battle
Forth have the children all gone,
Forth to the battle,
While on the lonely hill-farm
Toileth the father alone.

*36A. All the sons are gone,*
*gone to the garden (field) of war*
*Alone, an old parent*
*Guards his mountain field.*

37. In sunshine's brightness,
Or the gloom of cloudy days,
My only question
How, o'er hard or easy ways,
Fare the people, my people!

*37A. Shining- then gloom,*
*each time the clouds return,*
*my heart is heavy.*
*My people, like grass-*
*what will become of them?*

38. Awaking from dreams,
To my mind there first cometh
The question supreme
Of my soldiers what tidings
From the field of the conflict!

*38A. Waking from a dream,*
*my first thought-the warrior,*
*and how he'll meet the foe.*
*Will word ever reach me?*

39. To die is glory!
Yet before the soldiers' shrine,
All pale with waiting,
Low, in sacrificial tears,
Parents, wives and children kneel.

*39A. At the sacred shrine*
*They offer tears in place of incense*
*They all seem to pray*
*All awaiting his return*
*Parents, wife - and children too.*

40. I long for the time
When the earth at peace shall
Beneath a calm sky,
And they raise the cup of joy
Full of gladness unalloyed.

*40A. In quietness, the night is calm. This time is*
*longed for to raise the sake cup in joyful toast.*

41. Wide is the dwelling,
The dwelling in which men live,
Wide as the world's wide;
Yet narrow the hearts of men;
Alas, I but wonder why!

*41A. We walk through this wide world*
*Our lives brushing many*
*Why is it then*
*That narrowness arises*
*From the hearts of humanity?*

42. Would that my human
Heart, as the cloudless heavens.
Blue in their shining
Depths, through the boundless spaces,
Broad in its sympathy were.

43. Among the millions
Of my people, far and near,
To share a pleasure
Is, o'er every other joy,
One beyond all magnitude.

44. Those there be who toil,
Treading the frozen midnight,
While at ease I sit
Warm through the long night-hours
Close to my brazier fire.

44A. *In the full fertile world. Even those who toil
in the frozen cold find bright clarity- in repose
close to the warm fire.*

45. The moon, that shineth
On my hedge in fragrant flower,
As brightly shineth
On the fence of rustic rails
Near some humble cottage-door.

46. Warm by the braiser
Of kiri-wood I'm sitting,
Yet am I thinking-
How cold within his cottage
The poor man feels the wind blow.

46A.*By solid brazier,*
*I warm my idle hands*
*and drift in thought —*
*a freezing gale blows through the gaps*
*cooling the poor man's sleep hut*

47. As for a subject,
Much I grieve when now I see
My trusty fav'rite
Growing old and weak of knee,
Worn in service's loyalty.

47A. *Though long the years, my faithful horse*
*grows old — yet still I could not bring myself to*
*give him into another's hands.*

48. If there be error
In gentle intimacy
Of love to counsel,
The heart of loyal friendship
Grows ever nearer, dearer.

49. Though on the level
Well-known pathway of to-day
We lightly travel ,
Care is needed lest we fall,
Tripped by error's hidden stone.

50. On summer evenings,
While I wait the rising moon,
And garden plants are
Being watered, fresh and fair,
Anxious thoughts no more molest.

*50A. I sprinkle water*
*on quiet garden grasses—*
*the moon will rise soon.*
*On this summer evening,*
*nothing stirs the heart.*

51. The books of childhood,
Which of old I used to learn,
I read to-day and,
As their faded leaves I turn ,
Am a boy again, a boy.

52. Through hours of evening,
When from the busy oflice
Have gone the toilers,
Alone with heart of quiet
I read my volumes over.

*52A. True calm calls him so,*
*Dark and deep are evening's old glow,*
*Due calm clouds move east,*
*Cold old rooms hold quiet air inside,*
*Blue night folds into warm arms.*

53. The autumn evenings,
I rejoice to notice, now
Are growing longer,
So that I my books may read
Favorite volumes o'er an d o'er.

54. Many the papers
Officers eagerly bring,
Needing attention;
Yet my leisure still I find
Flowers to view with quiet mind.

55. Again in dreams, I
Dreaming quaffed from eager hand
The water springing
Pure from out the gleaming sand,
Shadowed cool 'neath bending pines.

*55A. In jet-black dreams tied,*
*cool dew gathers quietly—*
*beneath the pine's shade,*
*fleeting moments held by strength,*
*where time and silence embrace.*

56. Upon the autumn
Grasses, blooming where in days
Gone by I planted
Them within my garden ways,
Lonely gard'ners, silent, gaze.

*56A. That olden forest—*
*someone might walk it alone,*
*gazing as I did,*
*where once I gathered by hand*
*autumn flowers in the grass?*

57. I turn the mystic
Pages o'er; and joy to find,
Within their keeping,
Secrets, garnered in the past,
Opening wide the present's door.

*57A. In this present world,*
*comparing thoughts with the past,*
*Isonokami* [16]
*Sacred words left from the past-*
*Reading them is a delight.*

58. God must know my heart
That for the peace of the nations
Prayeth ever-,
For the sake of the people,
For the sake of the people.

59. As I older grow,
The teachings of my parents,
Deep within my heart
And deeper ever sinking,
Impress their truth profoundly.

60. Whene'er I treasure
Seek for thee, Fair Land of Reeds[17],
The richest jewel
Still I find, to meet thy needs-
People burgeoning with deeds.

---

16 Ancient Isonokami Shrine was built at nations start.
17 Ashihara no kuni," land of reeds" is a traditional name for Japan.

*60A. In the reed-filled land,*
*thinking to rule this country,*
*yet even the grass*[18]
*and the people, it is clear,*
*are the true treasures here.*

61. The soldier fighteth
For his country on the field;
He also serveth
Who at home doth ever yield
Fruits of faithful industry.

*61A. For love of the land,*
*there can be no second path —*
*on the field of war,*
*to stand or fall in stillness,*
*each involves true resolve.*

62. I know full surely
That with single heart our Land
Obeyed the bidding
Clear of those High Gods who rule-
Ancient Sires of men who live.

*62A. The countries people*
*all united in spirit,*
*have protected well*
*the teachings of all the gods*
*the guardians of our home.*

---

18 Grass is a reference to nature and or food plants eg rice.

63. Year by year I think
Of cooling mountain streamlets;
Yet when summer comes
I have no time of leisure
To draw their flowing waters.

*63A. Though years bring my fears,*
*still I gather mountain streams-*
*in their cool embrace*
*a quiet joy flows onward*
*Only calm and ease of self.*

64. Do thy duty first;
Then only may'st thou linger
In the shadow sweet
Of flowers that are shedding
For thee their balm and perfume.

65. The man on duty,
Standing at the vessel 's helm,
Must watch nor slumber,
Though the winds in zephyrs blow,
And the waves lie calm below.

66. The man who ruleth
Still should keep within his heart
A standard holy,
Set to guide the humbler folk,
Prone to follow not obey.

67. In summer, even,
Oft' I lie the short night through
In sleepless planning,
Burning still my study lights
While my Country's good I scan.

*67A. Even on summer nights,*
*I lie restless awake*
*Till the sky grows light*
*Very many thoughts arise,*
*For the sake of the world.*

68. The heat I felt not
When my mind with cares of state
Was taken wholly;
But in leisure hours of late
Prostrate, petulant I lie.

*68A. The affairs of state —*
*While only heard from outside,*
*I never ever thought*
*were difficult and intense,*
*Like standing in scorching heat.*

69. Beyond my watch-care,
God will guard that distant spot,
In light and darkness,
Where the mind of man knows not
What of ill may be its lot.

*69A. Though my sincere heart*
*Cannot reach that far off land*
*even to its ends -*
*Day and night, the ancient gods*
*Will surely protect it well.*

70. Oh God in heaven !
If there be a deed of sin,
Thy wrath to merit,
Punish me; the people spare,-
All are children of my care.

71. Not for grace of mine,
As one in heart they serve
Their country, but for those
Ancestors, high and holy,
Who rule benevolently.

*71A. That all of us serve*
*The spirit of the land*
*With a single heart —*
*It is because of the blessing*
*Of our ancestral deity.*

72. Our fathers ' precepts,
Handed down from ages past
By rulers holy,
Have become a Nation's treasure,
Held in reverence closely claspt.

73. Throughout Yamato
May there grow abundantly
That wisdom-yielding
Herb which springs from secret seed,
Pregnant in the heart of man.

*73A. From the noble heart,*
*with the heart as the seed,*
*let teachings like grasses*
*grow lush and strong*
*in Yamato, the land of islands.*

74. The roots of grasses
And of trees from foreign lands
With us shall flourish,
When with fost'ring care we tend
Daily the gardens of Japan.

75. Before the presence
Of the unseen Deity
May stand the mortal
Whose true heart 's sincerity
Guardeth from all fear of shame.

76. God of victory;
Thou wilt aid the army brave,
Fighting not for me,
But for mankind o'er the earth,
For the progress that shall be.

77. God Ise[19]! Hear
My life-long supplication:-
Peace forever send
Through me unto my people,
For this my reign empowering.

19 Ise Shrine (*Ise Jingū*) is one of the most sacred Shinto shrines in Japan.

# 5. Empress Shoken Waka

78. E'en in Palace,
Where shadows deep are lying,
Hot are the shadows;
What mountain's sunbaked pathway
Now toils my Royal Husband?

79. Unpolished lying,
Of what use are precious gems
And silver mirrors?
Still on learning's pathway steep
Toil alone brings fair increase.

80. The unpolished gem
No slightest lustre showeth
To prove it of worth;
The mind of man neglected
Reflects no light of wisdom.

*80A. If not polished yet,*
*The jewel's bright light won't appear,*
*The human heart too*
*Also just the same, it seems,*
*Needs care to shine brightly.*

81. Easily we brush
The fallen dust from garments
Gleaming white and fair;
But from the mind beclouded
How hard to sweep the shadows!

*81A. From sacred pure cloth*
*Visible dust on the robe*
*It can be cleansed*
*Sorrow of the troubled heart*
*Though invisible remains.*

82. Howe'er they fashion
To their slightest wish the flowers
Which deck the hair,
The fragrance of the bosom[20]
Alone is beautiful.

83. Gone beyond recall
Is the thing that has happened;
By thy breath let fall
Not a word that is thoughtless,
Like a leaf on the river.

*83A. Let the past pass by,*
*There's no need to chase its steps,*
*Fleeting words once said*
*Should not be scattered in vain-*
*Leave them to fall and vanish.*

84. When no man seeth
Thy silent, secret doings,
Be not neglectful;
Guard then thy conduct strictly,
Respect thyself in judgement.

---

20 Heart. Bosom keep the syllable count to 7.

84A. *Unseen by others*
*Let my own heart not waver*
*Without slackening*
*My own actions and conduct —*
*would that I could uphold them.*

85. Drain not to its dregs
The sweet wine-cup that floweth:-
The cup of the spring
With its bloom or of autumn
When the maple-fire gloweth.

85A. *In the spring flowers,*
*in autumn's crimson leaves,*
*Even the sake cup-*
*in moderation indeed*
*I wish for a place of shade.*

86. Whenever I hear
The good news of victory
In battle attained,
I think of our sailors brave,
Our soldiers at the fore.

86A. *Tales of the battle,*
*News of victory arrives—*
*Each time I hear it,*
*I think of those loyal souls*
*And feel for their precious lives.*

87. To heal the wounded,
Who for Country's sake have born
Sad blows and grievous,
Healing gifts beyond all thought
Must be poured forth lavishly.

88. That which becometh
Roof-tile or precious jewel,
As is the spirit
Having and holding it fast,
Such is the gold which men seek.

*88A. The person who has*
*a hearts longing or desire,*
*for a small pebble*
*transforms it into a gem*
*it becomes shining gold*

89. Learn first how to smile,
Like the cherries that blossom
In beauty so rare,
E'er they scatter dishevelled
By the storm-gusts that tear.

*89A. What may disturb me*
*I set aside for a time*
*Cherry blossoms bloom*
*First, I learned to smile at them*
*A habit I once was taught.*

90. E'en as the precious diamond,   when left unpolished,
No gem like lustre showeth,        its worth to token;
Nor good nor ill attaineth        the soul of mortal,
Apart from friendship's shaping,  life's crudeness broken.

E'en as the hands of time,      in their ceaseless circles,
Moment by moment measure       unending ages;
The mind of man, in ceaseless    endeavour striving,
Will reap at last in infinite       lore its wages.

*90A. Even a diamond*
*Will never shine its true light*
*If left unpolished.*
*People, shaped by those they meet,*
*Change for better or for worse.*

*Like clock hands turning,*
*Time flows without pause or rest.*
*With steady effort,*
*No skill remains out of reach —*
*Diligence makes all things done.*

91. As is water in a dish,       be it square or round,
Shaped according to that form,   by that nature bound;
So is man by those with whom    keeps he company
Shaped and moulded good or ill      for eternity.

Better than thyself select      friends of noble part,
Emulate their virtue true     from a sincere heart;
Spur thy spirit's lagging steed   over wisdom 's height,
Using them to strengthen thee     unto greater might.

*91A. Water shapes itself*
*To fit the form of its vessel,*
*So people's spirits,*
*Change with those they come to know —*
*Good or bad, they are transformed.*

*Choose friends better than self,*
*Drive your heart like a strong steed,*
*On learning's bright path,*
*Urged onward by steady will,*
*Together, growth will follow.*

92. Even the spring tide gales blow soft;
the impartial hand
Of righteousness protects fair
Shikishima's[21] land

93. Green is the constant pine[22]
and green the constant troth,
That binds the ruled
and rulers, making one of both.

94. Happy the land where
sovereign mercy is so great,
That all men live as kindly
neighbours in the state.

95. No ripple stirs the pond
within the garden there:
Troubles shall ne'er disturb
the peace of our glad year.

---

21 Shikishima means Japan. Written in 1872, a year after Shoken's marriage.
22 The evergrreen pine tree symbolises longevity and prosperity

96. Like the sun goddess,
lured by Tachikara's skill[23]
From heaven's dark cave,
the morning sun peeps
o'er yon hill.

97. At night I sit, and looking o'er the fields,
Think of the myriad poor,
and all their toil,
And, as I think,
my sleeve is wet with tears.

98. The jewel in a lady's coronet
Gleams in her hair,
and sparkles in the gloom,
and yet 'tis nought, - a sparkle, not a light.
The book whose page enlightens the dark
mind is the true treasure.

99. Why should I fear
the harsh reproof of men
When my own conscience sparks
no word of blame?

100. Take heed unto thyself: the mighty god
That is the soul of nature, sees the good
and bad that man in his most secret heart
Thinks by himself, and brings it to the light.

---

23 The sun goddess hid behind the moon and was put back in place by Tachikara.

101. The winter, with its rigours, touches not
Our bodies, clad in vestments warm and rich;
But when we think upon the shivering poor
That freeze in their thin rags, the cruel tooth
Of pitiless winter bites our inmost heart.

# 6. One Line Summary Waka Index

## Meiji Tenno Gyosei

### Chapter 3
-. If we are all kin, why the turmoil?

### Chapter 4 – 77 Meiji Tenno Gyosei
1. Heartfelt speech heard once is never forgotten.
2. In the depths of my heart, words of light shines forth.
3. A clear sky reflects a tranquil heart, bathed in radiant light.
4. The truth in our hearts mirrors the heart of God.
5. Heartfelt sincerity makes even an ogre weep.
6. I'm swept along like pebbles in a fast, shallow stream.
7. The onward flow of mind brings quiet comfort to a restless life.
8. Beautiful words reveal the true heart within.
9. Beauty of a mind is untouched by thought.
10. Born to go forward, I carry echoes of the past.
11. In baby's scribble, the promise of learning shines.
12. May all, no matter the burden, rise to the strength of youth.
13. Timber holds the hush of hands long gone to silence.
14. Humble shelter, quiet soul.
15. Spared once, learn well. The path forgives, not forgets.
16. Small things, left unchecked, can grow into burdens.
17. When the guiding hand stops, disorder follows.
18. Whatever your purpose, let devotion be your grace.
19. Blaming others need not happen, if you own your mistakes.
20. Like the dawn, the heart rises, clear and bright.
21. A heart lifted, like a skylark, rises with hope into the spring sky.
22. There is always a path to the summit, if one chooses to climb.
23. After withstanding storm and snow the pine tree seems taller.
24. Falling raindrops never give up but hollow out stone.
25. A long wait fulfils a cherished purpose.
26. Even humble weeds may heal—if wisely chosen.
27. There is no lustre, I neglected to polished it.
28. Even in peace, the watchful heart must not waver.
29. Outside of battle never forget purpose, even in facing difficulty.
30. Make haste, go steady.
31. If we have no choice but to harm, we should still show mercy.
32. The soldier's slain honour easeth not parental grief.
33. Remember those who laid down their lives for our homeland.
34. The war beneath the moon.
35. Remember those who laid down their lives for our homeland.

36. The young garden the war, the old are left to guard the fields.
37. Clouds return — I fear for my people, like grass.
38. Woke from a dream—still no word of the warrior.
39. Tears offered at the shrine - they await his return.
40. Celebration
41. In vastness, it is the heart that confines.
42. May my heart be vast as the sky.
43. There is no greater joy than enjoying fun together.
44. From frost, light will emerge.
45. Moonlight touches flowers in gardens without distinction.
46. I'm warm, yet a cold wind freezes a poor mans sleep.
47. Too old to ride—yet I cannot give him up.
48. A true friend corrects you if you're wrong but stays by your side.
49. On the open road take care not to stumble.
50. A calm heart waits, trusting nature's flow.
51. Old pages open the heart to childhood.
52. In twilight's calm, old duties yield to quiet words.
53. Long autumn nights increase the joy of endless reading.
54. Though busy I pause to smell the roses.
55. The patient evergreen pine lets dreams and dew unite.
56. In the thicket many may see autumn flowers I once picked alone.
57. Old words enshrined bring joy into present times.
58. The divine alone knows a heart that whispers "peace".
59. Mother's words bloom brightly as the years go by.
60. People and nature are the nations treasures we call country.
61. Stand or fall, one path, one heart.
62. United our hearts guard sacred teachings.
63. Summer's cooling ease flows in mountain streams.
64. Ease in duty, restful peace in seasons of change, allows stillness.
65. Don't let go of the rudder even on calm seas.
66. Righteous behaviour allows both following and being led.
67. Sleepless planning for others sake.
68. Only in the fire do you feel the heat.
69. Where I cannot reach the gods protect.
70. If the people err, it is the ruler's responsibility.
71. By grace of the gods, in unity we serve.
72. Sacred speech, written and passed down is national treasure.
73. Let noble teachings take root and flourish.
74. Care brings even distant roots to bloom.
75. True sincerity is unseen yet unashamed before gods.
76. In cursed wars for world's sake, no god lends strength.
77. In prayers for peace our souls find ease.
    NOTE: Gyosei in Ch. 9 are numbered 104-106 as placed after
    Shoken Waka.

# Empress Shoken Waka in Chapter 5

78. From palace to heat, what mountain draws you?
79. Even brilliance needs polishing — so too the mind.
80. Unpolished, jewels and hearts stay dull.
81. Outer purity fades but sorrow lingers unseen.
82.True beauty blooms from a fragrant heart.
83. Let go. Don't waste words on the past.
84. Integrity in the unseen.
85. A quiet life amidst fleeting beauty.
86. Victory news brings feeling for fated precious lives.
87. Healing those who suffered for their country.
88. Heart makes the humble precious.
89. Pause to "smell the roses" (cherry blossoms), enjoy the moment.
90. We shine through learning and influence.
91. Shaped by others, choose your companions wisely.
92 Even nature can be harmonised by virtuous action.
93. Harmony through mutual commitment.
94. Neighbours dwell as kin in a land governed by kindness.
95. A still pond reflects the hush of a peaceful year.
96. Sun rises, light returns.
97. Tears of thanks for the toil of unseen hands.
98. Wisdom's light is a true jewel.
99. I fear no voice but my own.
100. Nature's soul reveals the heart's hidden truth.
101. Warmth pains the heart when others freeze.

# 7. Japanese Verses

1. Magokoro o
Utai agetaru
Kotonoha wa
Hitotabi kikeba
Wasure Zari keri.

2. Kumori naki
Kokoro no soko no
Shiraruru wa
Kotoba no tama no
Hikarinarikeri

3. Kumori naki
Hito no kokoro o
Chihaya furu
Kami wa sayaka ni
Terashi miru ran.

4. Me ni mienu
Kami no kokoro ni
Kayo koso
Hito no kokoro no
Makoto narikeri.

5. Oni gami o
Nakasu ru mono wa
Yononaka no
Hito no kokoro no
Makoto nari keri.

6. Sazare sae
Yuku kokochi shite
Yama kawa no
Asase no mizu no
Hayaku mo arukana.

7. Omou koto
Ari no mani mani
Tsuranuru ga
Itoma naki mi no
Nagusame ni shite.

8. Kotonoha no
Ue ui nioite
Yukashi ki wa
Hito no kokoro no
Hana ni zo arikeru.

9. Omou koto
Tsukurou koto mo
Mada shiranu
Osana kokoro no
Utsukushi ki kana.

10. Susumi taru
Yo ni umare taru
Unai ui mo
Mukashi no koto o
Mazu oshie nan.

11. Osanago no
Mono kaku ato o
Mite mo shire
Naraeba narau
Shirushi aruyo o.

12 Tsuku tsue ni
Sugaru tomo yoshi
Oibito no
Chitose no saka o
Koeyo tozo omo.

13. Kotosogishi
Mukashi no ie no
Tsukuri sama
Ima mo inaka ni
Nokori keru kana.

14. Sasayaka ni
Miyuru iei mo
Katatsumuri
Hitori sumu niwa
Koto tari nubeshi.

15. Ima wa tote
Manabi no michi ni
Okotaru na
Yurushi no fumi o
Etaru warawabe.

16. Tsumorite wa
Harau ga kata ku
Narinu beshi
Chiri bakari naru
Koto to omoe do.

17. Toki hakaru
Utsuwa no hari no
Tom osureba
Kurui yasuki wa
Hito no yono naka.

18. Yononaka wa
Takaki iyashi ki
Hodo hodo ni
Mio tsukusu koso
Tsutome nari kere.

19. Ten o urami
Hito o togamuru
Koto wa araji
Waga ayamachi to
Omoi kaesaba.

20. Sashi noboru
Asahi no gotoku
Sawayaka ni
Motamahoshi ki wa
Kokoro nari keri.

21. Akugaru ru
Hito no kokoro o
Hisakata no
Sorani sasoi te
Tatsu hibari kana.

22. Osora ni
Sobiete miyuru
Takane nino
Noboreba noboru
Nichi wa nari keri.

23. Yuki ni tae
Arashi ni taeshi
Nochi ni koso
Matsu no kurai mo
Takaku miekere.

24. Amadari ni
Kubomishi noki no
Ishi mite mo
Kataki waza to te
Omoi sute meya.

25. Omo koto
Tsuranukan yo o
Matsuhodo no
Tsukihi wa nagaki
Mono ni zo arikeru.

26. Ibuseshi to
Omo naka ni mo
Erabi naba
Kusuri to naran
Kusa mo koso are.

27. Shiratama o
Hikari nashi tomo
Oma kana
Migaki tarazaru
Koto o wasurete.

28. Yumi ya mote
Kami no osameshi
Kunibito wa
Koto naki yo nimo
Kokoro yurusu na.

29. Mi niwa yoshi
Hakazu nari temo
Tsurugi tachi
Toki na wasure so
Yamato kokoro o.

30. Muchi utaba
Momiji no edani
Furenu beshi
Koma o hikaen
Okagoe no michi .

31. Kuni no tame
Ada nasu ada wa
Kudaku tomo
Itsukushimu bek
Koto na wasure so

32. Kuni no tame
Taoreshi hito o
Oshimu nimo
Omowa oya no
Kokoro nari keri.

33. Yo to tomo ni
 Katari tsutae yo
Kuni no tame
Inochi o suteshi
Hito no isao wa.

34. Hashi i shite
Tsuki miru hodo mo
Tatakai no
Niwa no arisama
Omoi yari tsutsu.

35. Omo oedzu
Yo o fukashi keri
Kuni no tame
Taoreshi hito no
Monogatari shite.

36. Kora wa mi na
Ikusa no niwa ni
Idehate te
Okina ya hitori
Yamada moruran.

37. Teru ni tsuke
Kumoru ni tsukete
omo kana
Waga tami kusa no
Uewa ikani to.

38.Yume same te
Mazu koso omoe
Ikusa bito
Mukai shikata no
Tayori ikanito.

39. Kami gaki ni
Namida tamukete
Ogamurashi
Kaeru o machi shi
Oya mo tsumako mo.

40. Shizuka nimo
Yo wa osamar te
Yorokobi no
Sakazuki agen
Toki zo mataru ru.

41. Hiroki yo ni
Majiwari nagara
Ikanare ba
Sebaki wa hito no
Kokoro naru ran.

42. Asamidori
Sumiwatari taru
Osora no
Hiroki o onoga
Kokoro tomo ga na.

43. Chiyorozu no
Tami to tomo nimo
Tanoshimu ni
Masu tanoshimi wa
Araji tozo omo.

44. Fukura yo no
Shimo fumu hito mo
Aru mono o
Hioke ni nomi ya
Yori akasubeki.

45. Hagi no to no
Hana ni yadoreru
Tsuki kage wa
Shizu ga kakine mo
Hedate zaruran.

46. Kirihioke
Kakinade nagara
Omou kana
Sukim okaru
Shizu ga fuseya o.

47. Hisashiku mo
Waga kau koma no
Oi yuku o
Oshima wa hito ni
Kawara zarikeri.

48. Ayamachi o
Isame kawashite
Shitashimu ga
Makoto no tomo no
Kokoro nari keri.

49. Hirake yuku
Michi ni idete mo
Kokoro seyo
Tsumazuku koto no
Aruyo nari keri.

50. Niwa kusa ni
Mizu sosogase te
Tsuki o matsu
Natsu no yube wa
Omou koto nashi.

51. Shibaraku wa
Osana kokoro ni
Kaeri keri
Yomi narai nishi
Fumi o hirakite.

52. Tsukasa bito
Makadeshi nochi no
Yumagure
Kokoro shizuka ni
Fumi o mirukana.

53 Aki no yo no
Nagaku naru koso
Ureshi kere
Miru maki maki no
Kazu o tsukushi te.

54. Tsukasa bito
Sasaguru fumi wa
Okaredo
Hana miru hodo no
Hima wa arikeri.

55. Nubatama no
Yume ni futatabi
Musubi keri
Suzushi karitsuru
Matsu no shita tsuyu.

56. Sono mori ya
Hitori miruran
Mukashi Waga
Atsumeshi niwa no
Aki kusa no hana.

57. Ima no yo mi
Omoi kurabete
Iso no kami
Furi nishi fumi o
Yomu zo tanoshiki.

58. Chihaya buru
Kami zo shiruran
Tami no tame
Yo o yasukare to
Omo kokoro wa.

59. Tarachine no
Mioyano oshie
Aratama no
Toshi furu mamani
 Mini zo shimi keru.

60. Ashihara n o
Kuni tomasan to
Omou ni mo
Aohito kusa zo
Takara narikeru.

61. Kuni o omou
Michi ni futatsu wa
Nakari keri
Ikusa no niwa ni
Tatsu mo tatanu mo.

62. Kunitami wa
Hitotsu kokoro ni
Mamori keri
Tatsu mioya no
Kami no oshie o.

63. Toshi doshi ni
Omoi yaredomo
Yama mizu o
Kumite asoban
Natsu nakari keri.

64. Onoga jiji
Tsutome o oeshi
Nochi ni koso
Hana no kage ni wa
Tatsu bekari kere.

65. Nami kaze no
Shizuka naru hi mo
Funabito wa
Kaji ni kokoro o
Yurusazara nan.

66. Yononaka no
Hito no tsukasa to
Naru hito no
Mi no okonai yo
Tadashi kara nan.

67. Natsu no yo mo
Nezame gachi ni zo
Akashi keru
Yo no tame omou
Koto okushite.

68. Matsurigoto
Idete kiku ma wa
Kaku bakari
Atsuki hi nari to
Omowa zari shio.

69 Waga kokoro
Oyobanu kuni no
Hate made mo
Yoru hiru kami wa
Mamori masuran.

70. Tsumi araba
Chin o tsumi seyo
Amatsu kami
Tami wa wagami
Umishi ko nar'eba.

---

71. Kunitami no
Hitotsu kokoro ni
Tsukauru mo
Mioya no kami no
Mimegumi ni shite.

72. Tsutaekite
Kuni no takara to
Narini keri
Hijiri no miyo no
Mikoto nori fumi.

73. Muragimo no
Kokoro o tane no
Oshie gusa
Oi shigeraseyo
Yamato shimane ni.

74. Waga sono ni
Shigeri aikeri
Totsu kuni no
Kusaki no nae mo
Oshi tatsure ba.

75. Meni mienu
Kami ni mukaite
Haji zaru wa
Hito no kokoro no
Makoto nari keri .

76. Utsusemi no
Yo no tame susumu
Ikusa niwa
Kami mo chikara o
Soe zarame yawa.

77. Tokoshie ni
Tami yasukare to
Inoru naru
Waga yo o mamore
Ise no okami.

78. Omiya no
Uchi ni arite mo
Atsuki hi o
Ikanaru yama ka
Kimi wa koyuran

79. Migakazuba
Tama mo kagami mo
Nani ka s en
Manabi no michi mo
Kaku koso arikere.

80. Migakazu ba
Tama no hikari w a
Ide zaran
Hito no kokoro mo
Kaku koso aru rashi.

81. Shiratae no
Koromo no chiri wa
Harae domo
Uki wa kokoro no
Kumori nari keri.

82.Tori dori ui
Tsukuru kazashi no
Hana mo aredo
Niou kokoro no
Uruwashiki kana.

83. Sugi taru wa
Oyeba zari keri
Karisome no
Kotoba mo ada ni
Chirasa zara nan.

84. Hito no minu
Toki tote kokoro
Yur ub i naku
Mino okonai o
Mamori teshi kana.

85. Hana no haru
Momiji no aki no
Sakazuki mo
Hodo hodo ni koso
Kuma mahoshi kere.

86. Tatakai no
Kachi no tayorio
Kiku goto ni
Miikusa hito no
Mi o omou kana.

87. Ikanaran
Kusuri susume te
Kuni no tame
Itade oikuru
Mi oba sukuwan.

89. Motsu hito no
Kokoro ui yorito
Kawara tomo
Tama tomo naru
Kogane nari keri.

90. Midaru beki
Ori oba okite
Sakura bana
Mazu emu hodo o
Narai teshi kana.

91. Kongo seki mo
Tama no hikari wa
Hito mo manabi no
Yoki ni ashiki ni

Migakazu ba
Sowazaran
Tomo ni yori
Utsuru nari.

Tokei no hari no
Meguru ga gotoku
Hikage oshlmi te
Ikanaru waza ka

Tacma naku
Tokino ma mo
Hagemi naba
Narazaran.

92. Mizu wa utsuwa ni
Sono sama zama ni
Hito wa majiwaru
Yoki ni ashiki ni

Shitagai te
Nari nunari
Tomo ni yori
Utsuru nari.

Onore ni masaru
Erabi motome te
Kokoro no koma ni
Manabi no michi ni

Yoki tomo o
Morotomo ni
Muchi uchite
Susume kashi.

NOTES:

A. Japanese versions of Shoken Waka 93-101 are not provided as Romanji was not located.

B. Romanji versions of Gyosei 103-106 in Ch.9 are footnoted.

# 8. The Stillness Meditation System

*Many paths lead from*
*the foot of the mountain,*
*But at the peak,*
*we all gaze at the*
*single bright moon.*

*Rinzai Zen Master Ikkyu Sojun (1394-1481)*[24]

I keep on saying how Reiki and Stillness Meditation have a lot in common. This chapter will help to appreciate why. It may help you find things relevant to your Reiki practice.

## From Hypnosis to Meditation

For hundreds of years (at least), various people have noted that hypnosis is like meditation teaching and self hypnosis like solo meditation. For example, the hypnotist\teacher says to gaze at a candle. Or a lone meditator gazes at a candle. *NB: This reduces blinking that normally dampens the cornea. Airborne particles, insects etc can pass onto the eye. Never gaze at intense lights (eg. sun or lasers).*

Sir James Braid (1795-1860) kept a small shiny metal handle in his pocket. He got patients to stare at it held up close just above eye height. He named the resultant state "hypnosis", sometimes called Braidism. Usui Mikao said Reiki was not hypnosis.[25] He meant that Reiki was not Braidism rather than the broader range of states called "hypnosis" today. In Usui's day Braidism was seen as distinct from other methods of hypnotic induction.

Usui passed away in 1926. Ainslie Meares (1910-1986) studied medical hypnotism and psychiatry in the 1940s and his unifying theory of hypnosis and meditative states was published in the 1950s. Meares learnt many methods of inducing hypnosis using emotion, senses (visual, auditory, touch, movement etc), thinking and confusion. He used the best methods to help his patients. Along the way he gained international recognition and invented hypnotic art therapy, hypnotic clay modelling and the dynamic method of hypnosis. In general, he simplified his procedures over time. Initially, he used energetic touch as used in various schools since ancient times. This included non-contact gestures although he preferred hands on. By the time he had refined Stillness Meditation

---

24 Ikkyu's waka in Japanese was not able to be sourced. Hence the English version as presented in many locations has been quoted "as is".

25 Shin-Shin Kaizen Usui Reiki Ryoho Kokai Denju Setsumei 1928 and later.

teaching, there was minor use of voice for a few minutes (with some non verbalised phonation). Then, hands on touch to facilitate calm. Towards the end of his life, he largely abandoned use of voice but, some nonverbal phonation remained. Touch was emphasised.

Reiki works. Stillness Meditation works. Knowing it works allows one to help oneself and then others. Theory can help take things further. Both Meares and Usui agreed that "meditative touch therapy" can allow self healing of body, mind and spirit. All humans have the ability to heal themselves and others. Meares believed that Stillness Meditation was the mind's own natural method of restoring balance (also called homeostasis). Reiki, describes the strongly felt energetic flow. Meares' describes global relaxation. Let go. Let flow. Two sides of the coin - why Reiki and Stillness Meditation share a lot in common. I find myself on the strongest ground when I can see both sides of the coin apply. Unity in essentials.

## Meares' Visits to Other Systems

Dr Ainslie Meares regularly attended overseas psychiatric and medical hypnotist conferences. On the way to and from he stopped off at out of the way places to visit yogi, sufi, witch doctors, voodoo'ers, zen practitioners and all the rest. He verified his theory - meditation, hypnosis, mysticism related states involve a single universal state hidden inside a variable overlay. Meares visited the main schools all over the world, including in Japan. But, in Japan, Reiki was only practised in secret at that time. Takata Hawayo lineage Reiki arrived in Australia via Beth Gray in 1983, just before Meares passed away. Meares had no contact with Reiki. This allowed me the gift of finding it myself in recent times.

In Japan, a Zen Abbott told Meares he must kill himself. Being a compassionate psychiatrist from Western culture this was a shock - until he saw it was a saying (koan) about ego loss rather than suicide. After he returned to Australia, Meares began to write poetry, as he put it, a western approach derived from Zen.

Another example from his visits was an improved understanding of meditation progression. Both topics are discussed later.

## Types of Meditation

Dr Meares believed that all types of meditation are based on an underlying universal state with a variable overlay. In all types of meditation, the logic and critical faculties temporarily cease. The overlay might involve sensory, emotional or cognitive aspects of mind eg. chanting\mantra, visualisation, breathing, compassion and so on. If the overlay completely disappears this leaves just the underlying state - Oneness or Stillness. Meares did not deny

Stillness to others. He taught a simple, direct approach to this universal underlying state as he found it worked best. It is what worked best for me, too.

Reiki lineages that remained in Japan feel that mantras (kotodama), visualisation (eg. symbols) and so on are training wheels to be discarded later on. I feel this fits in quite well with loss of overlay to reveal the Still mind underneath. Some methods learn the overlay and then deliberately abandon it (the training wheels idea). Others, learn the overlay and inadvertently learn its loss. Having learnt the direct approach first may make this easier to see.

There should be unity in learning meditation. Yet, freedom of choice to use different methods. Training wheels too - until one is ready to travel down the path without them. Remember, that Usui Mikao, achieved much with neither attunement nor symbols. Just a human meditating on a mountain. His is a potent reminder that the ability to experience harmony and tranquillity lies within all of us.

## The Stillness Meditation System

Ainslie Meares didn't use the word pillar, as such. The things I call pillars are found in Meares' book *Relief Without Drugs* (RWD) and later books. The instructions in RWD are included in my book, *Ainslie Meares on Meditation*. RWD is the book Meares recommended for beginners who couldn't travel to see him.

The 5 pillars are:
1. Stillness meditation
2. Meditation progression
3. Being calm and at ease
4. Support factors
5. Touch therapy (aka meditation teaching, 1:1 healing)

I am grateful to other meditative touch therapy systems, like Reiki, for what I've learnt and also for helping to understand and better explain the 5 pillars system.

**Stillness Meditation**. This involves effortless global relaxation that transcends slight initial difficulty (or discomfort) whilst in a stationary symmetrical position during meditation practice. Sitting on a chair is a good place to start. Refer to *Ainslie Meares on Meditation* for Meares' detailed set of instructions.

One practices an identical type of Stillness Meditation:
- ◆ in solo meditation (pillar 1),
- ◆ during meditation progression (pillar 2) and in
- ◆ touch therapy (pillar 5) whether 1:1 or teaching a group. The recipient or group experience Stillness too.

**Meditation Progression**. *This book is for general information only (see p4).* Meditation progression involves the same effortless meditation but with tiny increments of difficulty gradually added over time. Relaxation in the presence of slight initial difficulty. Sitting on a chair. Laying on the floor. Other postures. There are other sorts of difficulty ("stimuli") too. Tiny amounts of difficulty gradually add up, over a long time, to profound relaxation in the presence of substantial difficulty.

Ainslie Meares had several decayed teeth removed, without anaesthetic, relying purely upon Stillness Meditation for pain control. The first, a decade after he started meditation practice.

Usui Mikao practised meditation, for who knows how many years, then walked up a steep slope and meditated without food on Mt Kurama for 21 days. Summer temperatures may drop to zero degrees Celsius and winter is subzero when snow falls. Usui is said to have been pushed by a Zen Abbott who told him to kill himself. The risks on Mr Kurama were high. Fortunately, Usui's transcendance led to profound tranquility AND he survived, shared his healing skills and this led to the worldwide spread of Reiki.

Lack of difficulty has its problems too. Easy comfort laying on a bed will send one to sleep rather than into meditation. These days, many people find they can relax the body but mental relaxation eludes them due to a lack of slight initial difficulty. Or, they meditate daily but plateau (ie. without pillar 3).

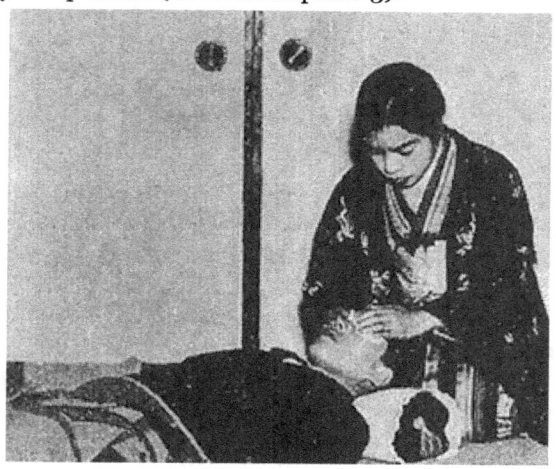

The above photograph was taken 7 years after Usui Mikao passed away for the book *Tomita-ryu teate ryoho* by Tomita Kaiji a student of Usui[26]. Western chairs and tables were rare in Japan until 1945.

Early Reiki practitioners knelt (seiza) with their recipients kneeling or laying down on the tatami floor as shown in that photo.

---

26 After Usui passed, Tomita left Usui's Reiki Association and formed his own.

Modern Reiki experts have been impressed by the results of early practitioners. At least part of it is due to pillar 3. But, only ever add tiny, safe amounts of difficulty gradually to meditation and healing practice. Tomita writes he endured extreme discomfort and could not stand up after his first one hour kneeling meditation. He experienced neurovascular compression and was lucky to avoid permanent peroneal or similar nerve damage.

It should be blatantly clear that too much difficulty (in single or multiple exposures) adds a risk of injury, illness or worse. This applies to both teacher - practitioners and their clients who all need full information, and possibly medical clearance, to make safe choices. Ainslie Meares' documented progressive postural and stimuli sequences are in *Ainslie Meares on Meditation*.

**Being calm and at ease.** This refers to one's state outside of meditation sessions. In daily living, one learns to be calm and at ease as one goes about doing things. Calm and ease that eventually persists in the face of discomfort or difficulty.

Sincere effortless diligence, experiencing calm and ease while facing difficulty, even great difficulty. The calm after Stillness Meditation flows onward ie. it persists for a period. It can be cultivated so that it stays with you more and more over time.

A completely Still mind cannot be maintained as you go about doing things. However, one can relax and be calm as you think, feel and move. All this can happen without effort or striving. Ease of mind. This is why many people practice and when the fruits of it arrive they are truly sweet to taste.

**Meditation support factors**. During our evolution we became adapted to the range of environmental conditions that prevailed. Our biology evolved to self adjust so as to be able to survive within certain limits. If we pass too close to these limits then our functioning is compromised. This can range from impaired quality of life, minor discomfort through to adverse health effect, even serious or fatal in extremes. For example, brain injury or death from hypothermia.

Without getting bogged down, the mental rest and integration from Stillness Meditation helps us cope and flourish. We can help Stillness Meditation work better by ensuring that we do not pass to close to those limits (see above). "*Meditation support factors*" can relate to a Still Mind and a Sound Body.

"Sound Body" factors include: sleep, sensible daily exercise, leisure, eating a diet that meets our nutritional needs and so on.

"Still Mind" support factors includes the facilitation of emotional evolution towards becoming more fully human. "Still Mind" support factors also includes poetry (see later). 11 of Meares' 35 books were poetry which says a lot about its value as a meditation supplement.

My book, *Still Mind Sound Body*, contains further details about the support factors.

**Touch therapy** refers to teaching Stillness Meditation to either a group (meditation teaching) or 1:1, also as therapy or healing treatment. In the 5 pillars system, those who learn meditation (but not teaching) learn 4 pillars (ie 1-4). By the time a person learns to teach using touch they are an experienced meditator. They have regular experience of Stillness in meditation and calm and at ease in daily living (pillars 1-4). This protects them from the negative emotions some healers experience during touch therapy. Stillness involves an absence of disturbance. So, disturbance is not unconsciously picked up (introjected) by the experienced one. Empathy continues to allow feeling what the recipient feels but effortless relaxation sheds any negative component. This also allows the unsettled meditator to calm down towards the teacher's state.

Self healing and self balancing are natural human abilities. They are facilitated by receiving touch from an experienced teacher. Meditation teaching and Reiju-attunement have quite a bit in common.

I've mentioned the use of nonverbal phonation during spoken guiding at the start of meditation class which mainly use touch. Kotodama has helped me understand non-verbal phonation better.

**A note on lost and shrunken pillars.** Sadly but with responsibility, I point out that some Stillness Meditation teachers don't teach all 5 pillars. Some teach as few as one or just a couple of shrunken pillars. Some have added or changed things that Meares would have tolerated but may not have approved of. Of course, what they teach works, but not as well as it might.

Freedom of choice is important. Complete information as a basis for fully informed choice is important too.

Now you understand a bit about the Stillness Meditation system, we can move on to discuss poetry.

# 9. Poetry and Meditation

## Introduction

Usui Mikao was teaching in 1922 after he came down from Mt Kurama. Waka recitation was in place before the first 100 Gyosei booklet was published in 1926. The booklet refers to Reiki Ryoho not <u>Usui</u> Reiki Ryoho, Usui is not mentioned.

On Usui's memorial stone, Gyosei are mentioned as Ikun (ethical testament). Then, the Precepts are outlined in detail. It seems a diplomatic way of putting Usui's emphasis on Precepts ahead of Gyosei and showing high regard for Meiji Tenno. Gyosei and the Precepts adds two rounds of recitation with overlap. For example, the Ch. 3 waka (seas and storms) overlaps with Precept 1 ("no anger"). Today, some lineages just recite the Precepts.

Gyosei became absent from the Reiki that left Japan with Hawayo Takata. A great many people learnt Takata Reiki without Gyosei. One can learn Stillness Meditation without poetry too.

There should be unity in essentials: learning meditative experience within both Reiki and Stillness Meditation. But, there is freedom using poetry as a support.

## Ways of Reading Poetry

Poetry can be approached using logic or aesthetics but not both simultaneously! One must pass from one mental state to another.

**Logic**. One can logically analyse a poem eg. meaning and clarity of words and grammar. Comparison with other literary works etc.

**Aesthetics**. Aesthetic experience requires a different approach. The poem must be felt rather than analysed. We read the words and let our mind freewheel its way to an impression. This is helped by experiencing mental relaxation so the mind can pass into a receptive state. The logical and critical faculties cease, the mind "contemplates" the poem, freewheels and poetic feeling is evoked. This freewheeling also helps learn Stillness Meditation (and Reiki).

**Unwanted effects of repetitious recitation**. Highly repetitious experience of sensory, emotional or cognitive elements, result in a monotonous dull state. The monotone persists and inhibits freewheeling and Stillness. Even if one stops repetition, it tends to echo and the mind remains stuck. Repetitive recitation can do it. In Usui's time, Braidism was known to be different to other methods collectively called hypnosis today – they had not identified the monotone. Note that the energetic touch used in Reiki and Stillness Meditation is quite different. Soothing. Not monotonous.

**Contemplation** describes experiencing a verse in a relaxed mental state. The logic and critical faculties are absent and the mind retains its full ability to freewheel and read between the lines.

**Freewheeling into uplift.** We read a verse and our mind freewheels. If the poetry is good we are uplifted. Negative poetry has the reverse effect. Here we limit our interest to poetry that uplifts. We can be uplifted by sadness depending upon how it is portrayed. In theatre, the heroine or hero's response to tragedy can uplift.

**Solo vs. group effects**. Poetry can be experienced solo or in a group. Reciting poetry in a group can be similar to a choir singing an uplifting song that leads to helpful feelings of calm and unity.

**Patriotic waka** tends to shift feeling in the direction of courage, determination and group coherence but away from calm. This is why some waka were removed from the Reiki booklets over time. After 1945, cultural change in Japan favoured further changes. A few patriotic waka are included in this book to show the full range.

## Tomita Reiki in 1933

In **stage 1** (joshin ho), Tomita[27] suggests purifying the heart-mind in kneeling while silently contemplating Gyosei. He says one identifies with and takes on the feeling portrayed by Meiji Tenno.

In **stage 2A** (hatsurei ho) one experiences the calm sensation all through but especially feels the relaxation (or flow) in the hands and navel (hara).[28]

In **stage 2B** Tomita outlines ways to facilitate "let go, let flow" ie. hands in prayer position, fingers clasped in lap and held slightly apart. He emphasises allowing the whole body to physically relax. So that later on relaxation and flow are better able to be communicated to recipients especially via relaxed hands.

Tomita does not mention the 5 Precepts, although it is clear he lived them himself. He provides 7 Gyosei for use in training. Three are in Ch. 4 ( 22, 24, 42) and the other four translate as follows:

---

27 Tomita K (1933). Reiki to Jinjutsu. Tomita Ryu-Teate Ryoho.
28 In terms of relaxation:
**Palms.** Relaxation in the limbs is due to reduced voluntary and sympathetic nervous system activity and is markedly felt in the palms (also face and feet).
**Navel.** Relaxation in the gut is primarily due to increased parasympathetic tone ("rest and digest"). For example, soft gut motion or subtle vibration, gentle gurgling, soft fullness, lightness and warmth. Of course, as relaxation expands it is all through your body and mind.

103. However it be,
Even if faced with troubles,
I will not give in—
This is my Shikishima's
living Yamato spirit.[29]

104. Which way shall I turn
In the blaze of the noonday sun,
this road burning white-
I seek the path that is right
just like the small, steadfast ant.[30]

105. Even if longer,
the path that people ought take,
if I walk that path,
I believe there will not be
danger upon that journey.[31]

106. Good and evil,
though one speaks of others' faults,
with easy words -
there was no such person who
reflected upon themselves.[32]

## Reiki Today

During Meiji Tenno's reign, there was no TV etc - only news papers and books. Photographing him was forbidden. Only 2 official photographs exist. Meiji Tenno was held in the highest regard by his people. There was mystery and revelation in reading the testament of this sacred descendant of the Sun spirit. He spoke to even the most humble reader through his waka. Many are aspirational - reflecting upon and suggesting ethical and spiritual improvement.

29 Ikanaran\ koto ni aite mo\ taymanu wa\ Waga shikishima no\ yamato damashii.
30 Izugata ni\ kokoro sashite ka\ hizakari no\ Yakutaru michi o\ ari no yukaran
31 Toku to mo\hito no yuku beki\ michi yukaba\ Ayuki koto wa\ araji tozo omou.
32 Zen'aku\ o hito no ue ni wa\ iinagara\ mi o kaerimiru\ hito makarikeri.

We must discuss them with great respect. But, times have changed and so has the position of Gyosei too. This is reflected in the reduction in numbers and usage of Gyosei in Reiki.

In modern classes, a sharing chat, an activity eg. selecting cards with chat etc. can allow the logical and critical faculties to slow and encourage a shift towards relaxation and the freewheeling state of mind. Next, the activity ends and meditation commences. Similar to how one passes through Tomita's stages (see above).

Gyosei can be read in a way similar to how poetry is used in the Stillness Meditation system ie. as a meditation support factor (pillar 4). Although, some western readers find Gyosei elusive and other verses like Ainslie Meares' poetry more accessible. Reading some of Meares' poetry can also provide practice that allows the option of working up to enjoyment of Gyosei later on.

## Stillness Meditation & Poetry

In teaching Stillness Meditation one uses some words at the start, but mainly nonverbal communication like presence, gesture, touch and nonverbal phonation. After verbal guiding has ceased, touch is used to help calm each individual. This also adds calm and unity within the class. Touch is very simple. It involves no words and so the mind can relax all the way to Stillness. Relaxation is letting go. Relaxation allows sensation, thoughts and feelings to dissolve until nothing remains. But, you dimly know you are awake and not asleep. There is an absence, or lack, of disturbance in the Still mind.

Mental activity involves the effort of networks of nerve cells firing tiny electrical signals to the next in the pathway (this achieves thinking, sensing, etc). As they relax, various nerve cells fire less and may cease firing completely. This provides them a temporary rest due to an absence of activity.[33] Hence, the calm feeling afterwards.

There are no verses without words. So, poetry can help to calm and allow group coherence somewhat but is limited by words. Nonverbal phonation involves sounds and so is closer to touch.

From the Stillness Meditation perspective, the mental activity of poetry reading and feeling are a form of overlay on the underlying state (see Ch. 8). When poetry is seen as overlay that prevents Stillness, it is clearly best read at times outside of Stillness Meditation. Uplifting poetry can give rise to a wonderful experience. But, even that is a result of mental activity as the mind is not Still.

The publication of *100 Gyosei* in 1926 provided waka to be used for Reiki purposes. Before that Gyosei had to be transcribed from other sources or memorised to use them in class. The 100 Gyosei book allowed practitioners to read them whenever they wanted.

---

33 Breathing and heart beat are self governed via the autonomic nervous system.

Ainslie Meares[34] encouraged his patients to read his poetry books: *"written in a kind of verse...in imitation of Zen writing. The significant point is that they are not intended to be logical... meaning comes from reading between the lines."*

Meares[35] goes on to point out: *"Patients are encouraged to leave the books lying about, to pick them up and read a few pages in the idle moment.* People told Meares that this *"added very greatly to their understanding of the meditative experience."*

People put the poetry book(s) on a workstation or similar place where it can be picked up and put down a couple of times daily. A poem or two are read and experienced here and there during the day. Poems are a supplement or support. If a student runs short of time then they practice Stillness Meditation for 15 minutes twice or thrice daily as a priority.

There should be unity in learning meditation and freedom in use of poetry. Whether you incorporate poetry into your sessions or separate poetry from meditation is up to you. However, if you put it inside sessions then consider how you will transition into meditation if you wish to experience the universal underlying state without overlay. Even the most beautiful poem results in overlay.

## Examples of Ainslie Meares' Poetry

Meares wrote 10 meditation poetry books – 11 if you count the 32 poems in *The Silver Years* which includes articles too. The rest of this chapter has some examples of Ainslie Meares' poetry. Book titles from which each poem was sourced are cited by footnote.

*Ainslie Meares on Meditation*, also has samples of Ainslie Meares' poetry as well as his good set of instructions which he continued to recommend to readers in later books.

*A Key To The Books of Dr Ainslie Meares* summarises the contents of 33 of Meares' books. That book was mainly compiled for researchers and Stillness Meditation teachers. It includes a first line index of all the poetry books. Meares' poetry books may be sourced in libraries or purchased from retailers.

34 Meares A (1982) Amer. J. Clin Hypn. 25(2-3): 114-121
35 Meares A (1982) Amer. J. Clin Hypn. 25(2-3): 114-121

Why have you come?

There is no reason,
Or none that I know.
I've just come.
And now I am here.

That explains all.
Heart to heart.
Soul to soul.
Together we make the journey.[36]


One is weak
And has little understanding,
The other is stronger
And perhaps
Understands a little better.
The stronger gives to the weaker,
But he does not give his strength
Or his understanding,
He merely gives something
That reawakens
The strength and understanding
Of the other[37]

36 Meares A. From the Quiet Place. p 10.
37 Meares A. A Way of Doctoring. p 8.

The "being with" of doctoring
Is to trust,
To expose ourself utterly
In the nakedness of our mind.
To explore
Beyond the experience
Of everyday living.
To allow our self the freeDialogue on Meditation
For our inner being
To commune
Soul to soul.
The one merges with the other
As days rests on the bosom of night
And night rides high on the crest of day.[38]


Why think
When thinking drives it away?

Yet, in moments of love or beauty
Glimpses comes to us
Of what perhaps it might be.

But in moments of stillness,
The glimpses come
With a clarity
We did not know before.[39]

---

38 Meares A. A Way of Doctoring. p 15.
39 Meares A. Prayer And Beyond. p 9.

Why keep talking of stillness.
When life is a matter of doing?

Go back.
Go back to where we went wrong.
This is the purpose of stillness.

Go back.
Then forward again on the new path.
Forward.
To what we could not reach before.

Go back.
More than thought and in feeling,
In being.
An new patterns of being arise.

Our body goes back in its being.
Faulty reactions are gone.
New ones arise in their place.
Healing can come,
When none could before.

This is the purpose of stillness.[40]

A little pebble is taken up.
Held, fingered, mused upon,
Has it not contributed
Something to our journey?[41]

---

40 Meares A. From the Quiet Place. p 47.
41 Meares A. Thoughts. p 19.

When we know
We cannot understand,
There dawns a light within us.

There comes an inward light
That shines as a star
In the darkening world of night.

It is clear again,
As water sparkles
In morning light.[42]

Sift the grain from the chaff
And there comes this other.

Thought without words,
Music without sounds,
Sight without image,
Love without body,
Prayer without words,

Come wind
Blow off the dross,
And leave me
With that which is more substantial.[43]

42 Meares A. Prayer And Beyond. p 40.
43 Meares A. A Kind of Believing. p 20.

A tranquil mind
Rides a fiery steed.

The calm within
Rides
The stress of the day.

Strive with ease
As in the marathon
Mile after mile.[44]


To sit, to be, to dream.
The idle hour
When so much is done,
When in stillness
And not knowing
We come to know.[45]


Invisible threads
Bind sun and earth,
Entwined
As you and I, my soul,
They journey onwards
Through all eternity.[46]

44 Meares A. A Kind of Believing. p 26.
45 Meares A. Thoughts. p 5.
46 Meares A. My Soul And I. p 10.

Awake, my soul,
The bell has sounded
That marks the birth of day,
And dawn
Has crept through the window
To scrape from our eyes
The scales of night.

The morning's sparkling dew drop
Joins with the air about her
And she is lost in a greater identity
To become a part of it all.[47]


We may call in our sleep,
But the angel of ease
Is deaf to our cry.
Beg her,
Kneeling,
She seems not to be there.
Entice her with some magic potion,
And she heeds it not.
Just leave open the door,
And little by little,
Like the light of dawn,
Her radiance
Comes to our being.[48]

47 Meares A. My Soul And I. p 20.
48 Meares A. Lets Be at Ease. p 7.

Who can separate cause from effect?
Health brings ease,
And ease brings health.
It needs ease
To experience something greater than ourself,
And the experience itself adds to our ease.
Are cause and effect
Simply manifestations
Of the same greater process?[49]


Feel the healing?

How can I feel it
We feel in different ways.
Feel the wind on your face.
Baby has never felt it.
Feel love, real love
It's beyond what the child can feel.
Feel that it's good,
Not everyone bothers to.[50]

Now feel the healing.

49 Meares A. Lets Be at Ease. p 33.
50 Meares A. Cancer Another Way? p 97.

# Epilogue

*Unity in essentials, freedom in non essentials and empathy in all things.*

I started out intending to present a collection of translated Meiji Tenno Gyosei and Shoken Waka for a wider audience. I found the time spent writing has helped me to look deeply into both Reiki and my Stillness Meditation system.

In deep meditation there is oneness, the void, emptiness, unity, loss of self, tranquility, serenity, harmony, peace of mind, an absence of disturbance, equanimity – all describe Stillness of mind. Yet, even in equanimity, empathy is enhanced and not bluntened.

Prudent progression in meditation can mysteriously deepen stillness. It is the transcendence of disturbing stimuli.

The learning experience of Stillness melded together with meditation progression allows an onward flow of calm and ease, even in the face of difficulty. Eventually, great difficulty. Calm and ease free one to live honestly towards one's purpose. It sounds like the path to *Anshin Ritsumei*.

Yet, a still mind depends upon a sound body too. Both still mind and sound body support factors help one to learn to meditate better and to enhance the onflow of calm and ease in daily living. Life gets better. And continues to get better. Here is where poetry fits. Reading beautiful poetry is leisure and a pleasure in itself. We are uplifted and the uplift allows us to life lighter and brighter. Reading poetry help us learn to free wheel into intuitive feeling and supports healing in the effortless relaxation of meditation.

Healing partner work and meditation teaching are basically the same – touch therapy. The only difference between partner work and teaching (or reiju) is the facilitator is highly skilled at relaxing into Stillness. The skilled one's calm becomes the calm of the group. Energetically, the skilled one helps the other to tune into a deeper flowing state. But, touch goes beyond the hands. When things go well souls sometimes touch.

To words, a bright light
Shining gently into heart
Echoing tones
Like spring wind that softly sings
To beauty or poetry[51].

51 Owen Bruhn, 3 March 2025, the day after a deep meditative experience.